The Grand Tour of
GREEK
MYTHOLOGY

Written and Illustrated by Mike Indovina
Edited by Melissa Rogalla

SATYR

PLAY

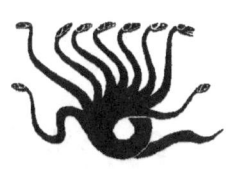

PROLOGUE PART 1

Now there exists an island across the wine-dark sea, where happy, joyous satyrs indulge in revelry.

So, just what is a satyr? I think you'll surely ask, their grinning satyr faces just like a comic mask.

Two goat-like horns adorning their shaggy satyr heads, and hooves right where their feet should be, and tails, or so it's said.

These spirits of the woodland protect each bird and beast between their merry antics and their hearty satyr feasts.

WINE

PROLOGUE PART 2

But as the satyrs frolicked, one spotted something new, someone, it seemed, had washed ashore; one said, "I wonder who?"

"Looks like a human girl," their leader then exclaimed, "Now tell me girl, where are you from, and what have you been named?"

The girl looked quite startled, as she viewed them one and all, and in answer to his question said, "I really don't recall."

"If your memory has left you," the satyr leader said, "then join us all for supper, and rest your weary head."

"Now I am called Silenus. A satyr of great fame. And we shall call you Pyrrha. It seems a lovely name."

PROLOGUE PART 3

And after they
had eaten, then
Pyrrha she
inquired,
"Can this all be
reality, all this
that has
transpired?"

"If creatures
such as satyrs
do really walk
the earth,
Then what of all
I thought I knew,
now what's it
really worth?"

"They say
the start of
wisdom," Silenus
answered back,
"Is admission
of one's
ignorance, the
knowledge that
we lack."

"Many mouths
will have to tell
it, if the whole
truth's what
you need.
I can give you
just one version,
I can merely sow
the seed."

"You will have my
wondrous tale,
told with perfect
skill and timing,
But for now, my
lovely Pyrrha,
let us cease
this senseless
rhyming."

IN THE BEGINNING

HEY, THERE'S A WEDDING RING AROUND URANOS!

Now first there was Chaos -- a teaming mass of everything and nothing. A fertile void from which sprang Gaea, goddess of the earth. With her awesome power, she created Uranos, god of the heavens, and the two were wed.

But, another god had forced his way into existence. His name was Eros -- the god of love and desire. With Eros around, it wasn't long before Gaea and Uranos had populated the universe with all manner of beings -- the results of their union.

These new creatures were monstrous -- giants of incredible size and matchless strength. Among these were the Cyclopes (one-eyed giants), the Hundred-handers (who, as their name implies, had 100 hands), and the Titans.

THE BIRTH OF VENUS

But, despite his great power, Uranos was afraid his many children would try to overthrow him, so he kept them all imprisoned deep within the earth.

Gaea would have none of this, so she fashioned a sickle of pure adamant and gave it to her son Cronus, one of the Titans.

With this weapon, Cronus struck his father, and the blood spilled upon the earth.

From the blood sprang many new beings. Enormous giants, lovely nymphs, and the vengeful Furies.

One of Uranos' more important parts fell into the sea near the island of Cyprus. From the sea foam arose Aphrodite, goddess of love and beauty.

IT'S APHRODITE... WITHOUT HER NIGHTIE!

IN THE MOUTH WITH BABES

Having usurped his father's position, Cronus was now the ruler of the universe.

Like his father, Cronus feared being overthrown, so each time his wife, Rhea, gave birth to a child, he would swallow it whole.

Finally, Rhea bore Zeus, and fearing this new child would meet the same fate as his siblings, she devised a trick.

She wrapped a large stone in the child's blankets, and gave it to Cronus. Thinking it his son, he gulped it down without hesitation.

Rhea brought Zeus to a remote cave on the island of Crete, where he was raised to adulthood by lovely nymphs, all the while planning his revenge on Cronus.

A TITANIC STRUGGLE

Now Zeus was ready. He freed the Cyclopes and the Hundred-handers from their imprisonment, and he tricked Cronus into vomiting up his brothers and sisters.

The Cyclopes forged powerful lightning bolts as weapons for Zeus, and together this band of gods and giants waged an epic war with Cronus and the Titans.

The Titans were defeated, and Zeus and his siblings became the supreme beings, ruling the universe from atop Mt. Olympus.

Zeus gave rulership of the sea to his brother Poseidon, and lordship over the Underworld to Hades. His sister, Hera, became his wife and queen of the gods.

I'VE GOT THE WEIGHT OF THE WORLD ON MY SHOLDERS.

HEPHESTUS' THRONE

Hera had a child named Hephestus. Unfortunately, her son was deformed, with misshapen legs and club feet. Disgusted, she hurled the infant from Mt. Olympus.

Hephestus was rescued by Thetis, a sea goddess, who raised him in secrecy. Over the years, Hephestus became a master craftsman and blacksmith, never forgetting the wrong done to him and his mother's poor parenting skills.

Finally, he plotted his revenge. He sent a beautiful throne to Hera. Delighted by the gift, she sat upon it, and was immediately bound fast. Even the mighty Zeus could not free her.

Hephestus was allowed to return to Olympus on the condition that he set his mother free.

THE GOD FATHER

Great Zeus fathered many children.

One day Zeus fell victim to a massive head-ache. Hephestus split his head open with an axe, and Athena, goddess of wisdom and strategy, arose, fully armed and armored, from the wound.

Zeus also fathered the twins Apollo and Artemis by the Titaness Leto. Apollo was the god of music, healing, and prophesy. His sister was goddess of the moon and hunting.

Oddly enough, Zeus actually did have a son by his wife, Hera. This son was Ares, god of war.

By the nymph, Maia, Zeus had another son. Hermes was his name -- a cunning trickster and god of messengers, travellers, and thieves...

ATHENA ALWAYS COMES OUT A-HEAD.

'TIL THE COWS COME HOME

When Hermes was only hours old, he stepped out into the world to explore. From the shell of a dead tortoise he built a musical instrument which he called a lyre.

Making music did not hold his attention for long, however. He soon came up with an idea to play a trick on his brother, Apollo.

Hermes stole Apollo's herd of cattle, and led them to a secret location, driving them backwards to add even greater confusion.

But, Apollo would not be fooled for long. With his powers of prophesy, he soon tracked down his thieving brother.

Hermes returned the cattle and gave Apollo the lyre as a gift. From this moment on, the two were great friends.

ZEUS VS. TYPHON

Gaea sought revenge on Zeus for overthrowing her son Cronus, so she spawned a terrible monster named Typhon.

Typhon headed towards Olympus, fathering many other horrible creatures along the way. When the gods saw him coming they fled to Egypt. Zeus, however, stayed behind to deal with the threat himself.

The battle between Zeus and Typhon was terrible -- taking the two all over the known world. Zeus hurled his lightning bolts with such fury that the thunder blasts could be heard even in the lowest regions of the Underworld.

Finally, Typhon was defeated, and Zeus imprisoned him in a part of the Underworld known as Tartarus.

PROMETHEUS BOUND

The Titan Prometheus was the creator of all animals, including men, who were his favorites. He gave them intelligence, and taught them many useful skills in order to better their lives.

The gift of fire, however, was reserved for the gods and the gods alone. This rule didn't stop Prometheus -- he stole the wondrous gift and presented it to his creations.

Zeus was outraged by the Titan's defiance, and ordered that he be punished at once.

Prometheus was chained to a mountain, where each day a giant bird would come and peck out his liver -- which would then grow back so the punishment could be repeated the next day.

EVE OF DESTRUCTION

To offset the gifts given by Prometheus to mankind, Zeus told Hephestus to create a new being named Pandora, the first woman. The other gods joined in by giving her, as gifts, various detrimental traits.

Epimetheus, the brother of Prometheus (who was not so wise as his sibling), took her as his bride. Her dowry was a large chest which she had been told never to open.

Pandora, having apparently been designed to be overly curious and given to temptation, opened the box. From it sprang all sorts of unspeakable evils to plague mankind for eternity.

But, inside the box, one thing remained. Hope.

NOW THAT'S THINKING OUTSIDE THE BOX!

THE RAIN OF ZEUS

The evil of mankind had become too great for the gods to bear, so Zeus decided it would be best to simply wipe them off the face of the earth. to serve this purpose, he created a massive flood which engulfed the entire world.

Prometheus, however, having anticipated such a thing, instructed his son, Deucalion, to build a ship so he and his wife might escape destruction.

When the flood had subsided, Deucalion and his wife, Pyrrha, had survived, but were alone.

The goddess Themis told them to pick up a handful of rocks and throw them over their shoulders -- which they did -- and as the rocks hit the earth, they transformed into human men and women.

THE BRIDE OF HADES

Hades was lonely down in the Underworld, and decided to take a wife. One day he spotted Persephone, the daughter of Demeter. Overcome by her beauty, and lacking anything resembling subtlety, he snatched her away.

Demeter was grief-stricken. She searched the earth for any sign of her missing daughter, and in her sorrow, neglected her duties as goddess of fertility and agriculture. Plant life all over the world withered and died, and the land became cold and barren.

Zeus finally stepped in. He ordered that Persephone be restored to Demeter, but for only two thirds of each year -- since she had tasted a pomegranate while in Hades' realm.

APOLLO AND ARTEMIS

Apollo, being the god of prophesy, wanted to establish his own oracle so mankind could take advantage of his great wisdom and knowledge of the future.

He chose an area known as Delphi, which was haunted by a fierce dragon called Python. He slew the dragon and founded a new city where his oracle could reside, and deliver his prophesies to mortals.

Meanwhile, Apollo's twin sister, Artemis, had eyes for Orion, a great hunter. So great was her love that Apollo feared his sister would violate her vow of virginity.

But Orion was a braggart. He boasted that he would one day hunt down every living creature on the face of the earth. Gaea, goddess of the earth, could not let this come to pass, so she sent a scorpion to deliver a fatal sting, and Orion met his fate.

PERFECT IO

Io was a mortal woman of great beauty -- so great that she attracted the attention of Zeus himself. But, as Zeus appeared to her, Hera, his wife, came looking for him. Not wishing to be caught with yet another woman, He transformed Io into a cow.

Hera was so taken by the beautiful cow that she begged her husband for the animal as a gift. Zeus had no choice but to consent.

Hera placed Io in her sacred pasture guarded by Argus, a creature with 100 eyes.

Saddened by the thought of Io spending the rest of her days as a cow, Zeus sent Hermes to play an enchanted song on his Lyre, and Argus was overcome by sleep. And so, Io was rescued and returned to her human form.

YET ANOTHER LOVE OF ZEUS

EGAD!
THIS ZEUS CAN'T SEEM TO
KEEP HIS LIGHTNING BOLT IN HIS
PANTS, CAN HE?

Europa was the daughter of Agenor, a Phoenician king. So lovely was she, that Zeus, as was the custom for the mighty sky god, saw fit to take her as one of his innumerable mistresses.

So, Zeus transformed into a beautiful bull. The beast looked so inviting to Europa, that she climbed on its back, and was quickly swept away to the island of Crete.

By Zeus she bore three sons: Minos, who was to become the most powerful ruler of Crete; Sarpedon, who would live several generations and fight with the Trojans in the Trojan War; and Rhadamanthys, who, along with Minos, would become a judge in the Underworld after his death.

CADMUS FOUNDS THEBES

Cadmus was ordered by his father to find his sister, Europa, who had been carried off by Zeus. He set off with little hope of success.

Finally, he came to Apollo's famous oracle at Delphi, and was instructed to abandon his search and build a new city at a location where he saw a cow lying down. Eventually he found such a place.

He sent some of his men for water, and when they didn't return he found that they had been devoured by a dragon. He killed the beast, and in accordance with Athena's advice, planted its teeth in the ground.

When he had done so, armed warriors sprang up from the earth. With these new allies, Cadmus built the city of Thebes.

REED MY LIPS

Pan was the god of shepherds and the son of Hermes. His goat-like legs and horns so frightened his mother that she ran away, but Hermes displayed his son proudly on Mt. Olympus.

One day, Pan spotted a nymph of extraordinary beauty. Her name was Syrinx, a virgin huntress, who found the god's advances unwelcome. She ran away, with Pan in hot pursuit, and when the came to a river which she couldn't pass, she transformed into a bed of reeds.

Disheartened, Pan picked some of the reeds, fastened them together, and created a musical instrument known as the Syrinx or panpipes, on which he played a mournful tune.

THE GOD OF WINE

Semele, daughter of Cadmus was another one of Zeus' many lovers. When she asked that the god grant her any gift she asked, he agreed. The gift she requested was to see Zeus in his full godly form.

Zeus knew what would happen, but he could not convince Semele to take back her request. Her stubbornness proved fatal, for she was burned to a cinder by Zeus' fiery glory.

But she had an unborn child, which Zeus recovered and stitched up into his thigh until it was ready to be born. This child was the god Dionysus.

Zeus gave the infant to Silenus to be raised on Mt. Nysa. Silenus, a wise satyr, tutored the child and became his dearest friend. When grown, Dionysus invented a new beverage which he called wine.

COMEDY OF EROS

Psyche was a princess of such great beauty that the people of her kingdom abandoned the worship of Aphrodite. The goddess asked Eros to avenge her by making Psyche fall in love with a hideous monster.

The lovely girl was swept away by a strong wind and came to a palace --home to her new husband -- who she could never see, for the palace was always kept in total darkness.

Psyche was determined to lay eyes upon her husband, so while he slept, she lit a small lamp and held it up to his face. It was Eros! But, a drop of hot oil spilled on his shoulder, and he woke up and ran away, clutching his wound.

Aphrodite demanded that Psyche perform various impossible labors in order to win back her husband. She had to sort huge piles of various types of grain, bring back a jar of water from the river Styx in the Underworld, and fetch a box of Persephone's beauty ointment -- All of which she accomplished.

Finally, Eros retuned, and the two lived happily forever after.

WILD WOMEN

Having grown old and tired, Cadmus turned over the throne of Thebes to his grandson, Pentheus.

Pentheus disliked the wild rites of the god Dionysus, and decided to outlaw them altogether.

A mysterious stranger appeared and advised him against this course of action, but Pentheus remained firm, and arrested the stranger, as well as a group of faithful bacchants (worshippers of Dionysus).

Mysteriously, the prisoners escaped, and Pentheus determined to find out just what went on during these secret rituals.

Hiding in a tree, he spied on the rites, but was discovered. Inspired by Dionysus with madness, the bacchants pulled the hapless Pentheus from the tree and tore him limb from limb.

PERSEUS, SON OF ZEUS

Acrisius, king of Argos, locked his daughter Danae away in an impregnable cell, for it was foretold that should she ever have a son, the child would one day kill him. This didn't stop Zeus, who visited her as a shower of gold, and soon she gave birth to Perseus.

Acrisius locked them both in a chest and cast it into the sea. After several days, the chest washed ashore on the island of Seriphus.

When Perseus was grown, Polydectes, king of the island, wished Perseus out of the way, for he wanted to marry Danae and he knew the boy would oppose such a union. The clever king devised a trick.

He demanded a tribute of horses from his subjects. Perseus, who owned no such animal, foolishly promised he would bring any other gift for which the king asked. Polydectes asked for the head of Medusa the monstrous Gorgon...

25

GOING, GOING, GORGON

The Gorgons were vile creatures -- so hideous that one look would turn any mortal being to stone. Perseus could never have accomplished this task had he not received help from Athena.

Her advice allowed the boy to obtain magical weapons to aid him in his endeavor: a sword, a shield, winged sandals to fly, and a helmet, which when worn would render its owner invisible.

Looking only at her reflection in his shield, Perseus beheaded Medusa and flew off.

On his way home, Perseus rescued the lovely Andromeda from a sea monster and the two were wed.

Finally Perseus returned and found that, in his absence, Polydectes had forced Danae to marry him. Angered, Perseus uncovered Medusa's head and turned the cruel king to stone.

THE MIDAS TOUCH

THIS ONE'S A GOLDEN OLDIE.

Midas, a king of Phygia, poured wine into a spring from which the wise satyr, Silenus, often drank. When Silenus stopped to quench his thirst, he was overcome by the wine and fell asleep. It was by this trick that Midas forced Silenus to impart his wisdom.

Finally, Midas returned Silenus to Dionysus, and the god was so happy to be reunited with his friend that he granted Midas his heart's desire: that everything he touched would transform into solid gold.

At first Midas was delighted, for his new power brought him unending wealth, but he soon learned that even his food and drink would turn to inedible metal the second they touched his lips.

To save the king from starvation, Dionysus took back the gift of the golden touch.

AN EAR FOR MUSIC

But Midas did not learn his lesson. While witnessing a music contest between Apollo and Pan, he insulted Apollo's musical abilities. For this, the god transformed Midas' ears into those of an ass.

Only Midas' barber knew his secret -- and would never reveal it, having been threatened by the king with fatal consequences.

The burden became too much to bear, so the barber dug a hole and muttered the forbidden knowledge into it -- then filled it in, thinking the secret safe.

On that very spot a patch of reeds grew, and to this day, when a gentle breeze blows through them, the reeds can be heard to to whisper, "Midas has the ears of an ass."

OEDIPUS ABANDONED

Laius, king of Thebes, was advised by the Oracle that should he ever have a son, that the child would one day kill him. Perhaps having heard the tale of Perseus (who did in fact accidentally kill his grandfather as the prophesy foretold), Laius was quite disturbed.

One day, his wife Jocasta had a son. Remembering the oracle, he ordered that the infant be taken by a shepherd and left in the wilderness as food for wild beasts. To make matters worse for the child, he pierced its ankles, to make escape even less likely.

The shepherd, however, had a kind heart, and couldn't carry out the king's command. He gave the child to another shepherd, who in turn gave it to Polybus, king of Corinth. Polybus raised the child as his own, and named him Oedipus, which means "swollen foot," because of the wounds on his ankles.

CENTAUR OF ATTENTION

In the city of Iolcus, Pelias usurped the throne from his brother, Aeson, who was the rightful king.

To protect his son, Jason, Aeson sent him away in secret to be raised by Cheiron, the learned centaur, on Mt. Pelion.

The centaurs were a tribe of creatures who were part horse and part man. Mostly they were savage and uncivilized, but Cheiron was very wise -- perhaps the wisest of all living beings. He raised Jason and trained him to face the difficult tasks which would surely lie ahead.

Cheiron trained many heroes. Asclepius, the expert healer, was a student of his, as were many others.

Meanwhile Heracles, son of Zeus, was trained by many great warriors and became an expert in the arts of wrestling and archery.

PEGASUS AND THE CHIMERA

Having been banished from his homeland, Bellerophon came to the city of Tiryns. There, the king's wife tried to seduce him, but he refused -- so the queen went before her husband and accused the young man of trying to seduce *her*.

Not wishing to harm a guest, the king sent Bellerophon to Lycia with a note for King Iobates (his wife's father). Iobates read the note which asked him to dispose of its carrier.

Iobates sent Bellerophon to kill the Chimera, a foul three-headed fire-breathing monster. Athena gave the hero a golden bridle with which to tame Pegasus, a fabulous winged stallion.

Riding on Pegasus, Bellerophon had no trouble slaying the Chimera. But the victory went to his head. He tried to fly Pegasus to Mt. Olympus to join the gods. Pegasus threw him off, and poor Bellerophon was forced to wander as an outcast for the rest of his days.

RIDDLE OF THE SPHINX

Oedipus, now fully grown, received an oracle which foretold that he would kill his father. Not wishing to do so, he left home -- thinking his adoptive parents to be his real ones.

While traveling, a noble looking man tried to force Oedipus off the road. He attacked and killed the man, which, unknown to him, was Laius, his real father.

Now Oedipus came to Thebes, a land being ravaged by a monster known as the Sphinx. The creature asked Oedipus a riddle: What walks on four legs in the morning, two at midday, and three at night. The clever wanderer answered, "man, who crawls, then walks, then leans on a cane."

Enraged, The Sphinx threw herself into the sea, and Oedipus won the hand of Jocasta, the recently widowed queen of Thebes.

HERACLES AND THE LION

Heracles was the son of Zeus, and an unequaled warrior. Despite his greatness, he was given to fits of insanity. During one such attack, Heracles accidentally killed his wife.

The hero went to the Oracle to learn how to be purified of his crime. She instructed him to go before King Eurystheus of Mycenae, and willingly submit to whatever labors he should assign.

This would not be easy, for Eurystheus had a knack for inventing impossible tasks. The first was to kill the Nemean Lion, a beast who was immune to all weapons.

Heracles defeated the monster by strangling it. He then removed its skin and wore it as an impenetrable cloak.

THE HYDRA'S VENOM

The next Task assigned to Heracles by Eurystheus was to kill the Hydra, a nine-headed serpent who dwelled in a nearby swamp. Whenever one of the monster's heads was severed, two would grow in its place.

Heracles was able to defeat the beast by having a companion immediately cauterize the wound whenever he managed to cut off one of the heads.

Having slain the Hydra, Heracles laced his arrows with its deadly venom. This was a powerful weapon, but also quite dangerous to his friends.

Once while battling savage centaurs, Heracles accidentally shot Cheiron. Being immortal, the wise centaur didn't die, but had to live in agony caused by the potent venom.

JASON AND THE ARGO

Jason, who had grown into a powerful youth, now returned to Iolcus to confront Pelias and retrieve the throne of his father. Pelias offered to step down if Jason would only perform a certain task: bring back the golden fleece from the kingdom of Colchis.

This was a dangerous task, for Colchis was on the far end of the world, but Jason accepted the challenge.

The young Jason invited Greece's greatest warriors to join him on his quest. Many came to his aid, including Orpheus, the great musician, Castor and Pollux, Peleus, and even Heracles.

A shipbuilder named Argus built a strong ship which was named the Argo, and Jason and the Argonauts set sail.

ARGONAUTS' ADVENTURES

The Argonauts had many dangerous encounters on their way. They battled cruel six-armed giants, and faced the women of the island of Lemnos, who had killed their husbands and seized control of the land.

To make matters worse, Jason lost his most powerful ally: Heracles. While stopping for supplies, Heracles' companion Hylus was abducted by a sea nymph while taking a drink from a local spring. Heracles searched everywhere for his friend, but could find no trace.

While Heracles searched, Jason set sail, oblivious to the fact that Heracles and Hylus were not aboard. The Argonauts would have turned back, but Glaucus, a sea god, instructed them to continue, for Heracles still had many labors to complete.

AMAZING DAEDALUS

There lived in Athens a great inventor known as Daedalus. After accidentally causing the death of his student, Talus, Daedalus was forced to flee the city with his son Icarus.

The two came to the island of Crete, where King Minos immediately hired the famous craftsman to perform a much needed task.

Minos was in possession of a savage monster known as the Minotaur -- half bull and half Man. He needed a place to hold the beast, and since the creature had a taste for human flesh, its home had to be inescapable for both the monster *and* his dinner.

Daedalus designed a building unlike anything that had ever existed: an intricate labyrinth with winding corridors that would baffle even the cleverest of men.

CLASHING ROCKS

Jason and his men were still far from completing their voyage.

In the land of Thrace, they encountered an old seer who was plagued by filthy creatures called harpies. They chased away the monsters, and in return, the seer, whose name was Phineus, advised them on the best route to Colchis.

Unfortunately, the only way to reach their destination was to sail through the Clashing Rocks, which would crush any vessel that attempted to navigate between them.

One of Jason's men sent a dove through the rocks, causing them to crash together. As the rocks parted again, the Argonauts rowed for their lives, and just barely made it through the deadly straits in time.

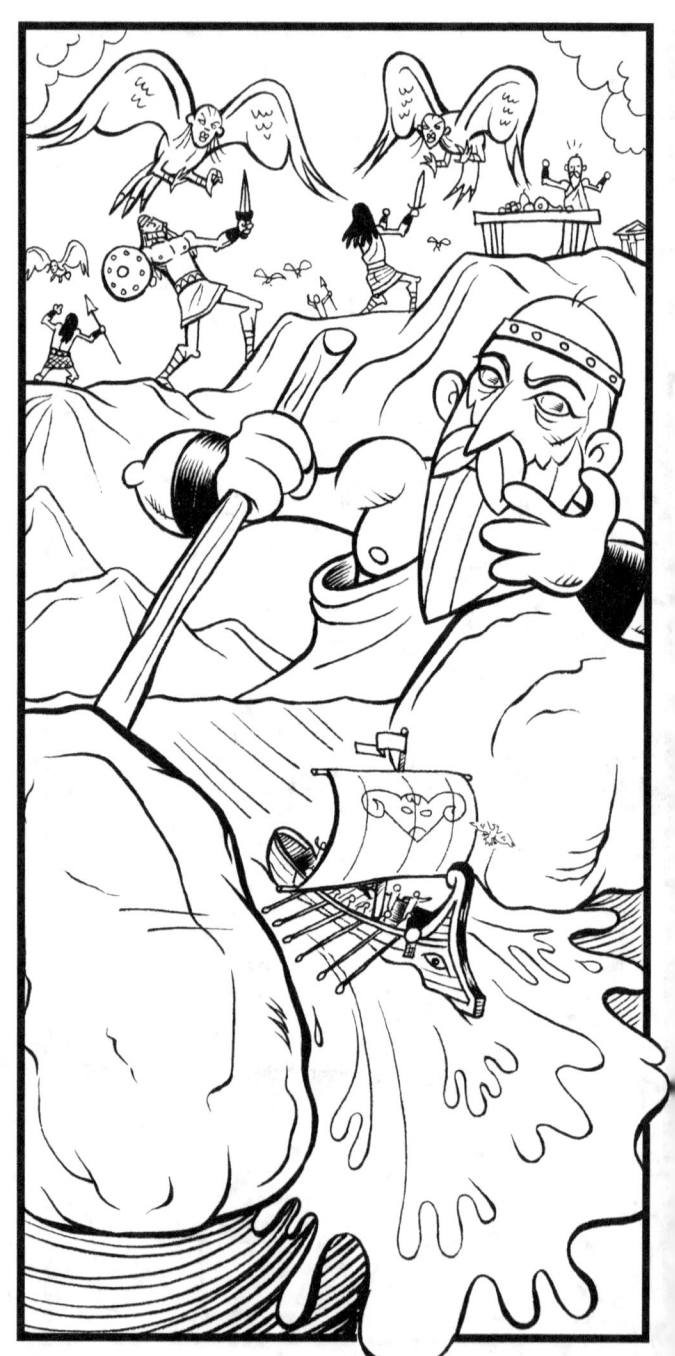

GOLDEN FLEECE

Finally, Jason arrived in Colchis. King Aeetes agreed to let Jason take the Fleece if he could successfully yoke his two fire-breathing bulls, plow a field, and plant a bag of dragon's teeth.

The sorceress Medea, Aeetes' daughter, fell in love with Jason and gave him a magic ointment which would make him temporarily invulnerable.

When Jason had planted the teeth, armed warriors sprang from the earth. Jason threw a rock into their midst, as Medea had advised, and the warriors immediately turned on each other until they were all dead.

Medea then led Jason to Ares' sacred grove, where the fleece was guarded by a foul dragon. Medea put the beast to sleep with a magical potion and Jason seized the fleece, escaping with Medea to the Argo. At last, the Argonauts were on their way.

HERACLE'S LABORS

Heracles still had many labors to complete before he could be purified for the accidental murder of his beloved wife.

He was ordered by Eurystheus to kill the Stymphalian birds who shot arrow-like feathers; to capture the Cretan Bull, who had fathered the savage Minotaur; to steal the girdle of Hippolyte, the Amazon queen who led an army of powerful female warriors; and to capture the cattle of Geryon, a giant possessing three torsos and a two-headed watchdog named Orthrus.

Each task was more difficult than the last, but Heracles triumphed again and again, proving himself to be nearly invincible.

PROMETHEUS UNBOUND

Heracles' most difficult labor yet was to steal the golden apples of the Hesperides.

The Hesperides were Nymphs -- beautiful maidens who guarded the sacred garden of Hera. But they were not alone. A gigantic dragon named Ladon also kept watch over the valuable prize.

Naturally, Heracles triumphed over the monster and collected the apples with the aid of the Titan Atlas.

On his way home Heracles came upon Prometheus, still bound to a mountain as punishment for stealing the gift of fire. Heracles felt sorry for the unhappy Titan, so he set him free. Zeus allowed this to happen, for according to him, Heracles could do no wrong.

RETURN OF JASON

For Jason and his Argonauts, the trip home was not without peril. Fortunately, they had the sorceress Medea to lend a hand in difficult times.

They faced the bronze giant Talos -- and were forced to sail between two deadly sea monsters named Scylla and Charybdis.

When they arrived home, Medea tricked King Pelias, claiming that she could rejuvenate his youth. Instead, her treatment resulted in the king's death.

For the murder, Jason and Medea were banished from Iolcus, and the throne went to Pelias' son, Acastus.

So, apart from the glory he had won, Jason's famous quest had been in vain.

CALYDONIAN BOAR

Angered by the Calydonian King Oeneus' neglect to give her a proper sacrifice, Artemis sent a giant boar to ravage the land, kill men and livestock, and otherwise make itself a nuisance.

Meleager, the king's son, led a grand hunt for the beast, and many of Greece's best huntsmen joined in. The greatest of these was, in fact, a hunts*woman* by the name of Atalanta.

When the party finally faced the boar, Atalanta shot it with an arrow, then Meleager finished the job. At last, the monster boar was slain.

Meleager, who was in love with Atalanta, gave the huntress the boar's skin as a gift, causing much ill will among the sexist huntsmen.

ORPHEUS AND EURYDICE

Orpheus, the great musician, who had voyaged with Jason aboard the Argo, was married to Eurydice, a lovely Nymph.

One day, while walking through the forest, Eurydice was startled by Aristaeus, the god of bee-keeping. the amorous god approached her, and she ran away, not wishing to receive his attention.

But, in her haste, Eurydice stepped on a poisonous snake and was delivered a fatal bite.

The local Nymphs punished Aristaeus for this misdeed by killing his entire colony of bees.

Orpheus was so grief-stricken by the loss that he determined to travel to the Underworld and bring his wife back.

ORPHEUS' DESCENT

As Orpheus descended into the depths of Hades' realm, his beautiful music attracted the shades of the dead. Even the boatman, Charon, gave him passage across the river Styx without his usual fee. And the three-headed dog Cerberus let the godlike musician pass without incident.

Finally he reached the palace of Hades. The god was so charmed by Orpheus' music that he decided to release Eurydice on the condition that, on his way back to the surface, Orpheus never look back to make sure she was following.

But the temptation was too great. When the surface world was in view, Orpheus looked back, and Eurydice was swept back to the land of the dead.

MEDEA'S REVENGE

Having failed to win back his throne, Jason sought to marry the princess of Corinth, Glauce, despite the fact that he was already married to Medea (who had betrayed her father to aid him in his quest for the golden fleece).

Medea's rage was deadly. With her sorcery, she killed Glauce and her father, the king. She then murdered her two children by Jason and escaped aboard the chariot of Helios, god of the sun, who was her grandfather.

Now a ruined man, Jason returned to his once proud vessel, the Argo, which was now old and rotten. As he pondered his past glory, a timber broke loose from the ship and fell on poor Jason, killing him at once.

THESEUS OF ATHENS

At age 16, Theseus moved a large boulder and found a sword and a pair of sandals which had been left there by his true father, Aegeus, king of Athens. So he decided to travel to the grand city and claim his right as heir to the throne.

Anxious to win himself glory, Theseus took the most dangerous rout imaginable, a road plagued by bandits and villainous giants, all of which met their end at his hands.

Medea, who was now the wife of Aegeus, wished to dispose of the youth so her own children would inherit the kingdom. She gave the boy some wine in which she had mixed a deadly poison.

But before he could drink, Aegeus recognized Theseus' sword and knocked the goblet from his hand. The king welcomed his new found son.

LABYRINTH OF CRETE

Athens had been living under the power of King Minos of Crete, and was forced to send a tribute of seven maidens and seven youths as food for the Minotaur. Theseus decided to end this tyranny once and for all.

When the time came for another tribute, Theseus volunteered. When in Crete, Ariadne, daughter of Minos, fell in love with him. She gave Theseus a sword and a ball of string, telling him to unwind it as he navigated the Minotaur's labyrinthine home so that he could easily find his way out after killing the monster.

Theseus followed her advice, and, in a fierce battle, managed to kill the savage Minotaur. With his companions and Ariadne, Theseus escaped to his ship.

FALL OF ICARUS

POOR ICARUS.
IF ONLY THEY HAD
FLOWN UNDER A
WAXING MOON.

Deducing that Theseus' victory could only have been achieved with the help of Daedalus, the builder of the Labyrinth, Minos had the inventor and his son Icarus imprisoned.

The clever Daedalus would not be held for long, however. He built wings out of feathers and wax so that he and his son could fly to safety. He instructed his boy not to fly too close to the sun, or the intense heat would melt the wax which held the wings together.

Either Icarus simply didn't listen, or the euphoric sensation of flight proved too much to handle, causing him to forget his father's wise advice. In either case, Icarus flew too high, his wings melted, and he plunged into the sea.

THE BLACK SAIL

Not being a man of his word, Theseus abandoned Ariadne (who had betrayed her kingdom to help him) on the island of Naxos.

Before Theseus left for Crete, he promised his father to hoist a white sail upon his safe return in place of the black one that was currently in use.

Theseus simply forgot his promise, and when Aegeus spotted the black sail on the horizon, he threw himself from a high cliff, thinking his beloved son to be dead.

Theseus' ineptitude proved advantageous in some respects. He was now King of Athens.

And what of Ariadne? The god Dionysus discovered her on Naxos, and she became his immortal wife.

MINOS' SHELL GAME

Minos was determined to find Daedalus, so he devised a cunning trick.

He took a thread and a shell to the various Greek kings, telling them that if anyone could run the thread through the intricate shell, he would grant a huge reward.

When Minos came to King Cocalus of Sicily, his trick paid off. When Cocalus presented the threaded shell to Minos, Minos knew that Daedalus must have helped him, and was therefore being sheltered by the king.

Cocalus had no choice but to surrender the inventor, but Deadalus would not be taken so easily.

While Minos bathed, Daedalus ran boiling hot water into the tub, and Minos was instantly killed.

ATALANTA

Atalanta, the great huntress, wished to remain forever a virgin, though her father urged her to take a husband.

Finally she gave in. She proclaimed that anyone who could beat her in a footrace would have her hand. Those who failed would be put to death.

Despite the danger and the improbable odds (since Atalanta was the fastest runner in Greece), many suitors attempted to win her. Predictably, each one failed and was killed.

Hippomenes, however, finally did defeat the huntress. As he ran, he dropped some golden apples which had been given to him by the goddess Aphrodite. the greedy Atalanta stopped to pick up the apples, and thus lost the race.

WITH WARRIOR WOMEN LIKE THIS AROUND, I COULD GET XENA-PHOBIA

CENTAURS GO WILD

In the land of Thessaly, the Lapith king, Peirithous, unwisely invited some centaurs to his wedding with Hippodameia.

Before long, the centaurs became drunk and began to carry off the Lapith women, including Hippodameia.

A climactic battle ensued. The Lapith warriors battled valiantly. Theseus, the Athenian king, who was also present at the wedding, fought with them. The brutish tribe was at last driven from the kingdom.

Later Heracles encountered the centaurs while visiting Pholus, a centaur who, like Cheiron, was very wise. His uncivilized companions attacked Heracles, who drove them away. Pholus, however, was wounded by one of Heracles' poisoned arrows, and died an agonizing death.

OEDIPUS WRECKED

Thebes now faced a new plague, and Oedipus, the king, sent his brother-in-law Creon to the Oracle to determine the best course of action. Creon returned with the news that the Plague would be lifted if the killer of Laius, the former king, were to be uncovered and banished.

Oedipus interviewed many men, including the prophet, Teiresias. Slowly he began to assemble the intricate puzzle. To his horror, he discovered that he himself was the killer of Laius, and furthermore, that Laius was his true father! It was a simple deduction that since his wife, Jocasta, had been Laius' wife as well, that she was in fact his own mother!

Filled with shame, Oedipus put out his own eyes and banished himself from the city, assisted in his blindness by his daughter, Antigone.

HERACLES THE DOGNAPPER

At last it was time for Heracles to perform his twelfth and final labor, which was to capture Cerberus, Hades' three-headed dog.

Heracles made his way into the Underworld and discovered that his friend Theseus had been trapped there by Hades when he had attempted to abduct Persephone, queen of the Underworld.

Heracles rescued Theseus, and subdued Cerberus, and the three made their way to the surface world.

Having completed his labors, Heracles was now free of Eurystheus' rule.

WHO'S THE HERO?

It was determined that Oedipus' two sons, Eteocles and Polyneices, would rule Thebes on alternate years. Eteocles, however, refused to step down when the time came.

So Polyneices raised an army and attacked the city. Although the two brothers killed each other in battle, The attacking forces were driven away, and Thebes was saved.

Creon, the new king, proclaimed that the body of Polyneices would remain unburied -- as food for the birds. His sister, Antigone, couldn't let this happen, so she opposed the king and buried her brother.

For her defiance, Creon had her walled up in a cave. On the advice of Teiresias, the prophet, Creon decided to undo his punishment, but he was too late. He found that both Antigone and his own son, Haemon, had committed suicide.

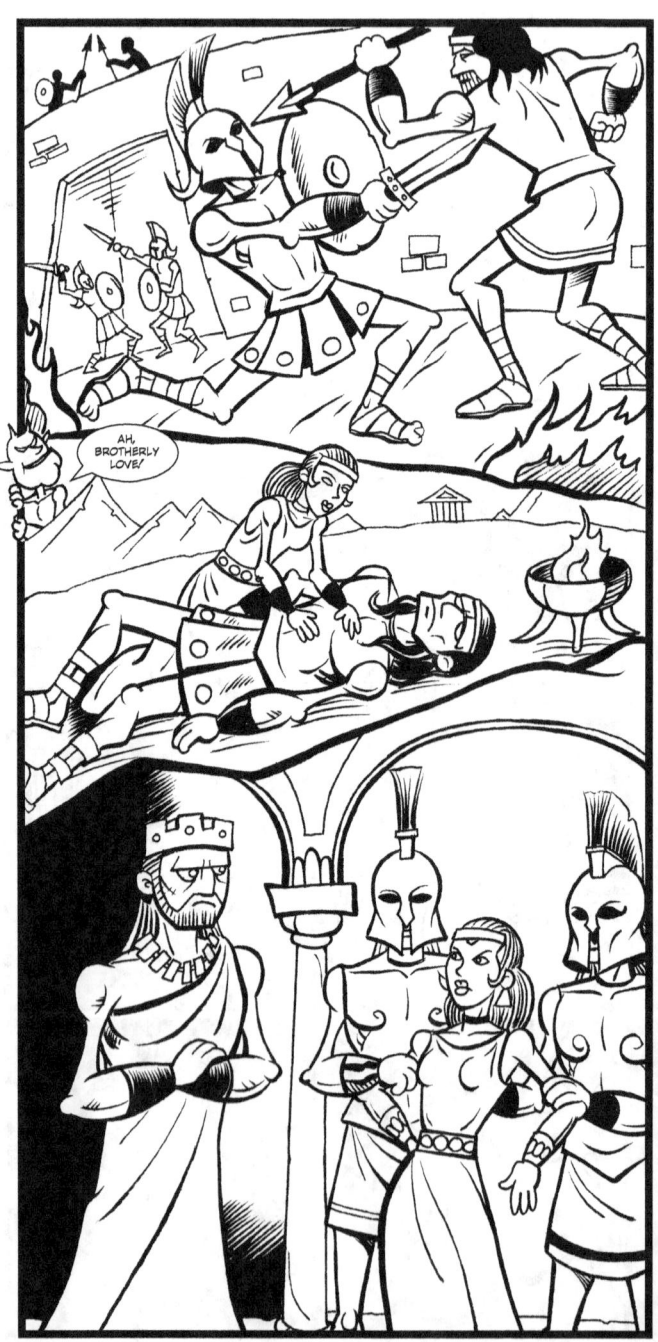

GODS VS. GIANTS

Still upset that Zeus had overthrown her son, Gaea sent her new children, the Giants, to attack Mt. Olympus. She instructed them on the where-abouts of a certain plant that would render them immortal.

Luckily, Zeus discovered the plan, and telling the sun to dampen his flame, found the plant himself in the darkness.

It was foreseen that the gods would only dcfcat the Giants with the aid of a mortal. For this purpose, Zeus recruited his son, Heracles.

It was a terrible battle. Zeus hurled his mighty bolts of lightning -- and Heracles made use of his deadly arrows. At last, the Giants were overcome, and Zeus' rule remained intact.

THE END OF HERACLES

When a centaur named Nessus tried to ravish Heracles' wife, Deianeira, the hero unleashed his deadly arrows, dipped in the venom of the Hydra.

As Nessus died he gave Deianeira some drops of his blood and told her to use it as a love potion should Heracles' love for her ever be in question.

When a time came that Deianeira feared that Heracles' affections were directed elsewhere, she soaked a new tunic in Nessus' potion, and gave it to her husband as a gift.

When Heracles put on the shirt, the Hydra's venom seeped into his body. The great hero suffered great agony, and finally died, a victim of the clever centaur's trick.

FOR THE FAIREST

It was prophesied that the goddess Thetis would bear a child greater than his father, so Zeus decided to marry her to a mortal. That man was Peleus, the former Argonaut.

At the wedding Eris, goddess of discord, placed a golden apple marked "for the fairest" where it could be easily found by the guests. Aphrodite, Hera, and Athena all claimed the prize, which started a monumental argument between the three goddesses.

Thetis soon bore a child who she named Achilles. Wishing no harm to come to her son, she dipped him in the River Styx in the Underworld. This made him invulnerable to harm everywhere on his body except for a small area on his left heel, by which the goddess held him.

APPLE OF PARIS' EYE

Zeus grew tired of the three goddesses constantly bickering over the ownership of the Golden Apple, so he chose Paris, a prince of the great city of Troy, to judge them in a beauty contest.

Each goddess bribed Paris with wondrous gifts. Hera promised him a happy marriage, Athena promised him great wisdom, and Aphrodite promised him the most beautiful woman in the world.

Paris chose Aphrodite, who in turn granted him the love of Helen, wife of Menelaus and queen of Sparta.

Helen was the daughter of Zeus, and the loveliest mortal woman who had ever lived. Paris left at once to claim his prize.

A THOUSAND SHIPS

So, Paris and Helen ran off together. When Menelaus discovered what had happened, he was furious. He came before his brother, Agamemnon, king of Mycenae (which was the most powerful city at the time).

Agamemnon and the other kings of Greece were all bound by a promise to protect Menelaus' right to Helen -- a pact they had made years previous when they were all suitors for her hand.

The Greek forces gathered in an area known as Aulis. It was an enormous fleet, the largest the world had ever seen. All the great kings and warriors were present, including Nestor, Ajax, Achilles, and Odysseus. For this, Helen's is widely known as the Face That Launched a Thousand Ships.

SEER OF EVIL

But, because of some offense, the goddess Artemis wouldn't let the Greek fleet set sail, sending only unfavorable winds.

Calchas, a great prophet, told Agamemnon that the goddess required the sacrifice of his daughter, Iphigeneia, or the Greeks would never set sail.

Agamemnon was grief-stricken. How could he kill his beloved daughter -- and what would be the consequences if he did not? Surely the Greek forces would take her by force, and his home and all his possessions would be lost as well.

Finally, he consented, inventing a story of a marriage with Achilles to lure his doomed daughter.

In the end, Iphigeneia went willingly, and Artemis secretly spared her life, whisking her off to her temple in the land of Tauria to serve as a priestess.

THE TROJAN WAR

And so the war raged on for ten years, but Troy's walls proved to be impenetrable to the Greek forces. In this time, Achilles proved to be the greatest of the Greek warriors and the mighty Ajax, the tallest of the Greeks, was nearly invincible as well.

In the tenth year, Agamemnon, the leader of the Greek army, confiscated a prize which Achilles had won through his great valor: a slave girl named Briseis.

Achilles was enraged, for he held the woman very dear and he had had quite enough of the High King's slights, so he decided to withdraw from the war altogether.

While the Greek forces were bombarded by the Trojan's unending assaults, the noble Achilles sat sulking in his tent, refusing rejoin the battle even after Agamemnon offered to return the girl and grant Achilles many grand gifts as well.

FURY OF ACHILLES

But, Achilles' great friend, Patroclus, donned the wondrous armor of Achilles and joined the battle. The Trojans, thinking him to be Achilles, were thrown into a panic. Hector, the greatest of the Trojan warriors, met him in battle, and soon Patroclus was slain.

When Achilles' learned of this, he was devastated and a great fury filled his heart. He raced onto the battlefield, seeking revenge for his lost comrade. Achilles and Hector fought with unequaled skill, but in the end, Hector was killed.

Achilles tied Hector's body to his Chariot and dragged it around to walls of Troy. Finally, however, he surrendered the body to Priam, king of Troy and father of the fallen Hector.

ACHILLES' HEEL

Soon after, Achilles met his fate when Paris shot him in the heel, his one vulnerable spot. The Greeks mourned the loss of their great hero by holding grand funeral games. To the victor would go Achilles' fabulous armor, which was made by the god Hephestus.

The powerful Ajax thought himself to be the most worthy, but he was defeated by Odysseus, the cleverest of the Greeks. Ajax was so overcome with anger and frustration at his loss that he slipped into an insane frenzy, attacking a nearby herd of livestock, thinking them to be enemies.

When he recovered, he was filled with shame. He placed the hilt of his sword in the ground so that the sharp point faced upward. He then hurled himself on the blade, and died instantly. Now the Greeks had lost their two best fighters. Victory seemed hopeless.

CLEVER ODYSSEUS

But the Greeks still had a great asset: Odysseus. His cunning and eloquence were well known throughout the world, and proved to be an indispensible resource.

Through his brilliant diplomacy, Odysseus secured two new allies: Philoctetes, who possessed the poisoned arrows of Heracles, and Neoptolemus, the son of Achilles.

The Trojans had in their possession a statue of Athena called the Palladium. It was said that any city which held this prize within its walls would be unbeatable. Odysseus once again proved his value when he snuck into the city and stole this priceless artifact.

Helen spotted the hero and recognized him at once, but for reasons of her own, she remained silent.

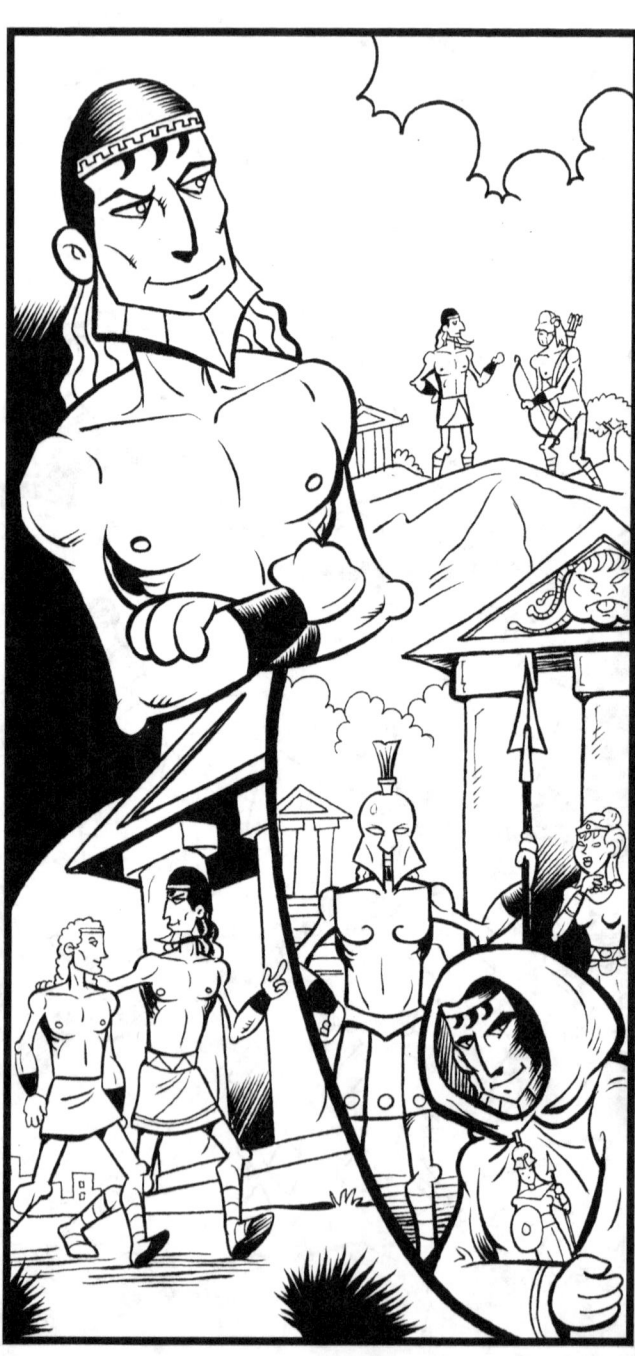

TROJAN HORSE

By far, Odysseus' greatest trick was the invention of the Trojan Horse. He built an enormous horse of wood and hid some Greek soldiers inside. He then advised the Greeks to set sail, and hide on the far side of a nearby island.

When the Trojans saw that the Greeks were gone, and had left this huge object behind, they wished to take it within their walls to commemorate their victory.

That night, the Greeks poured out of the Horse's innards and opened the gates to let the remainder of the army inside the city.

Taken by surprise, the Trojans were at last defeated, and the great city of Troy was burned to the ground. Only the Trojan hero Aeneus managed to escape with a small band of men.

The beautiful Helen was returned to Menelaus, and the Greeks departed with their heaps of Trojan wealth.

RETURN OF THE KING

While High King Agamemnon was away at Troy, his wife Clytemnestra plotted her revenge for the supposed death of her daughter, Iphigeneia.

When Agamemnon returned to Mycenae, Clytemnestra greeted her husband graciously. She invited him to take a bath and recover from his long journey, all the while burning with rage and secretly planning his demise.

Clytemnestra and her lover, Aegisthus, threw a net over the High King while he bathed. They then took his life, cutting him down with a deadly axe.

When an elderly slave heard Agamemnon's cries, he snatched the king's only son, Orestes, and carried him off to safety.

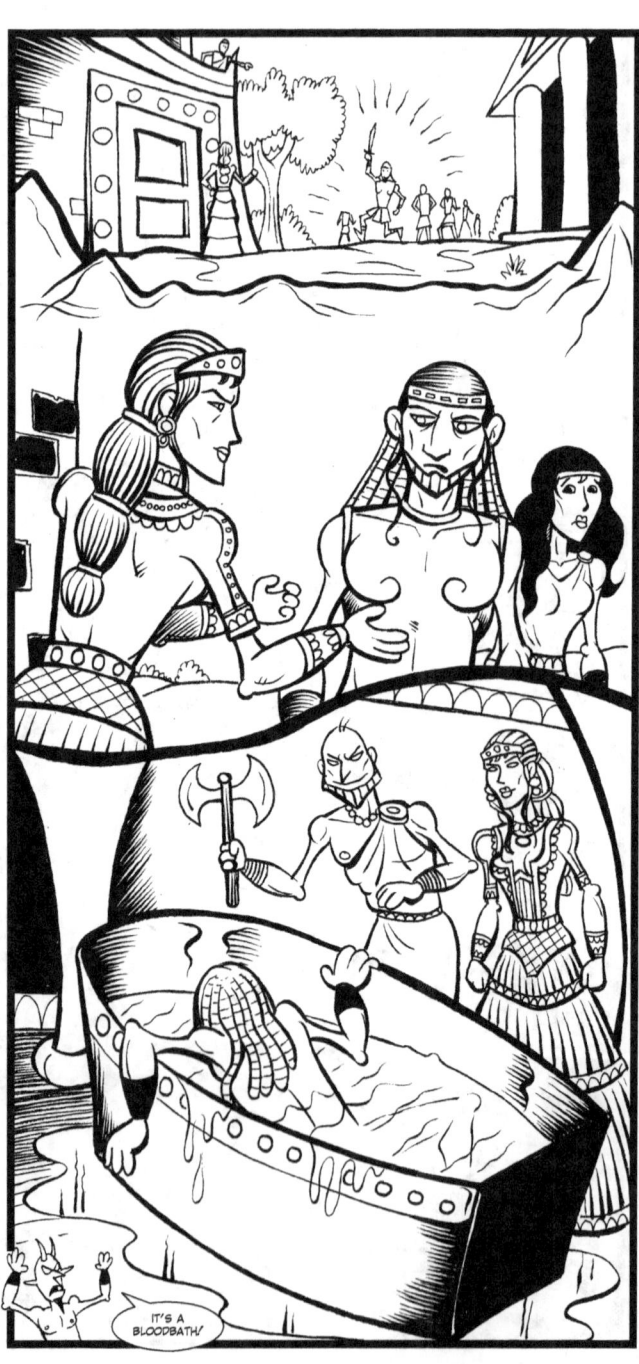

IT'S A BLOODBATH!

MENELAUS LOST

As Menelaus sailed home with his wife, Helen, he became hopelessly lost and arrived in the land of Egypt.

On the advice of the locals, Menelaus sought out a great prophet -- a sea god by the name of Proteus. It was said that anyone who could capture the god could force him to impart his endless wisdom and knowledge of the future. The task would not be easy, however, for Proteus could assume any shape he wished.

Menelaus grabbed hold of Proteus, and held him tight through his various transformations. Finally, the god surrendered, and showed Menelaus the way home.

At last, Menelaus returned to the great city of Sparta with his wife, and ruled until the end of his days.

ORESTES' MURDER

Orestes, now a young man, visited the Oracle to ask after his fate. He was instructed to return to Mycenae and kill his father's murderers: Clytemnestra, his mother, and her lover, Aegisthus. Naturally, this advice was not taken lightly by the boy. The killing of one's parents was considered one of the greatest crimes imaginable.

Still, he returned, and conspired with his sister, Electra, who had been married off to a commoner. Through cunning and treachery, the two murdered their mother and her lover.

This attracted the attention of the Furies, vengeful goddesses whose job it was to avenge crimes of blood. They pursued Orestes to the ends of the earth, driving him to the edge of insanity.

HELL HATH NO FURY LIKE A FURY'S SCORN!

LOTUS LAND

On his trip back from Troy, a massive storm had swept Odysseus and his men to the far reaches of the world. All hope of finding Ithaca, his beloved homeland, seemed lost.

Eventually he came upon an island. The inhabitants of this island lived off the sweet leaves of the Lotus plant, which stripped them of all motivation. They existed in a drug-induced stupor, and had no responsibilities, goals, or desire for anything except to once again taste the Lotus.

When some of Odysseus' men tasted the plant, they had to be dragged back to the ship, and Odysseus ordered his crew to set sail at once.

After several days, Odysseus landed on another island. He took some of his followers ashore to search for rations, but even the cunning Odysseus wasn't prepared for what he would find...

CYCLOPS VS. NOBODY

Odysseus and his party came upon a cave filled with vast amounts of cheese and goat's milk, but soon the gigantic master of the house returned and sealed off the exit. It was Polyphemus, the cruel Cyclops.

He quickly snatched two of Odysseus' men and gulped them down. Odysseus knew he would have to devise a monumentally clever ruse to escape his inhospitable host.

He introduced himself as "Nobody" and offered the giant some wine, which he had luckily brought along. Unused to the beverage, Polyphemus fell into a deep sleep. Odysseus then sharpened a large timber and drove it into the Cyclops' single eye.

Polyphemus screamed, "Nobody is killing me!" a plea which was not taken very seriously by the other Cyclopes on the island.

When the Cyclops unsealed the cave to let his sheep out to pasture, Odysseus and his men escaped by tying themselves underneath the oversized beasts.

ORESTES FORGIVEN

The Furies pursued poor Orestes as far as the land of Tauria, where the young man learned that his sister, Iphigeneia, was still alive and serving in the temple of Artemis. He snatched his sibling and ran off towards home.

By now, Apollo and Athena felt they should put a stop to this endless cycle of revenge, so they organized the very first trial by jury.

The elders of the great city of Athens listened intently to Orestes, and the cunning arguments submitted by Apollo, Athena, and the Furies themselves.

They found Orestes innocent, and he was free of the Furies' wrath at last. And so, Orestes returned to Mycenae and was hailed as its new king.

HOG HEAVEN

Poseidon now had good reason to hate Odysseus, for Polyphemus was his son. The god sent a great tempest, and Odysseus was helplessly tossed across the sea. Finally, his ship landed on a remote island.

He sent some men for supplies, but they didn't return, so Odysseus set out in search of his comrades alone. Just then, the god Hermes appeared. He told Odysseus that Circe the sorceress was master of the island and that she had transformed his men into swine. He then gave the hero a special herb that would make him immune to Circe's enchantments.

When Odysseus met the sorceress, she tried to transform him as well, but the spell failed. Threatening her with a sword, Odysseus ordered the witch to restore his men and let he and his party leave in peace. She agreed, and instructed the hero to visit Teiresias in the Underworld, who would advise him on the best route home.

WHERE'S ODYSSEUS?

Back in Ithaca, Penelope, Odysseus' faithful wife, was pining away for her lost husband.

To make matters worse, her home was overrun with suitors for her hand, for everyone believed the noble Odysseus to be dead. The boisterous group had long outstayed their welcome, and were slowly depleting Odysseus' wealth -- eating and drinking him into poverty.

to hold off the suitors, Penelope devised a trick. She announced that she would choose a new husband when she had finished a certain tapestry. Every day she wove feverishly, but by night she would slowly unravel her expert work so the tapestry would never see completion.

CAPTIVE AUDIENCE

On Teiresias' advice, Odysseus sailed on, but there were many dangers ahead.

The only way home was to travel between Scylla and Charybdis. Scylla was a six-headed monster who would snatch sailors with her ravenous jaws and gobble them up. Charybdis was a deadly whirlpool who swallowed whole ships, dragging them to the bottom of the sea. Odysseus was forced to choose the lesser of the two evils: Scylla. Mourning his lost comrades, he continued on.

The next trial was the Sirens. The Sirens would enchant men with their sweet songs and force them to crash on the sharp rocks which they made their home. Odysseus stuffed wax in his men's ears so they couldn't hear. Curious to hear the Sirens' songs, He ordered that he be tied to the mast, so he could listen, but would be helpless to act.

A SIX-HEADED MONSTER? THAT'S SCYLLA.

DIDO'S LOVE

The Trojan hero, Aeneas, who had escaped destruction at the hands of the Greeks, was ordered by the gods to found a new settlement -- which would one day become the greatest city the world had ever seen. Aeneas and his band had many bold adventures in their quest for a suitable location,

He came to the city of Carthage which was ruled by Queen Dido. Dido fell deeply in love with the noble hero, and he returned her affections, causing him to linger in the grand city for quite some time. Twice the god Hermes appeared to Aeneas in order to remind the hero of his sacred duty.

With sadness in his heart, Aeneas finally resolved to depart and seek his destiny.

Dido was so overcome with grief at her lost love that she hurled herself on a funeral pyre and died instantly.

CALYPSO'S BOY-TOY

Odysseus' men had defied his orders and slaughtered the sacred herd of Helios. For this the god destroyed them all. Only Odysseus survived -- and was washed ashore on the island of Calypso, a beautiful sea Nymph. She fell in love with the noble hero, and kept him captive for what seemed like an eternity.

Back on Ithaca, Athena, in the guise of a wise old man named Mentor, urged Telemachus, Odysseus' son, to prove his manhood by sailing to the mainland and asking the other Greek kings for news of his father.

HOMEWARD BOUND

Acting on behalf of Athena, Zeus sent Hermes, messenger of the gods, to command the lovely Calypso to release Odysseus at once. Sadly, the nymph helped Odysseus build a raft and sent him on his way.

After a rough trip, Odysseus was washed ashore in the land of Phaeacia. There, Princess Nausicaa discovered the wanderer, and presented him to her father, King Alcinous.

After hearing Odysseus' wondrous tale, the king ordered that one of his strong ships transport Odysseus home at once.

On the trip home, Odysseus was administered a drug which made him fall into a deep sleep. When he awoke, he found himself alone on the shores of Ithaca, his long lost homeland.

CLEANING HOUSE

Athena disguised Odysseus as an old beggar, and Telemachus, who had just returned from his excursion, escorted the old man to the palace, where the cruel suitors mocked the elderly stranger.

Now Penelope proposed a contest. Any man who could string Odysseus' powerful bow and fire an arrow through ten axe heads would have her hand in marriage.

All the suitors tried and failed, but the old beggar decided to have a go at it. He strung the bow and expertly fired a shaft through the axes. He then threw off his rags, and was at once revealed to be Odysseus, home at last.

With the aid of his son, he dispatched the suitors, and finally, after twenty long years, he embraced his faithful wife, Penelope.

ALL ROADS LEAD TO ROME

Finally, Aeneas reached his destiny, the land of Latium in a country known today as Italy. Having been advised by an oracle that his daughter must marry a foreigner, King Latinus welcomed the stranger.

However, Turnus, the ruler of a nearby tribe, had long hoped for the hand of Latinus' daughter. He attacked Aeneas and his men, and a massive war raged on.

At last, though, Aeneas defeated Turnus in battle, and plunged his sword into the rival warrior's heart.

Victorious, Aeneas built a new settlement, a small town which would one day be known as Rome, a city which would hold a vast empire, spanning the entire known world.

THE
END

 # GLOSSARY OF NAMES

Achilles: Achilles was the son of the goddess Thetis and Peleus, a former Argonaut. Thetis made him invulnerable by dipping him in the river Styx -- everywhere but the heel by which she held him. Achilles fought in the Trojan War, and quickly distinguished himself as the most powerful Greek warrior.

Aeetes: Aeetes was the king of a far off land known as Colchis. He was the son of the sun god Helios, and the brother of Circe. The sorceress Medea was his daughter. Aeetes possessed a great treasure known as the Golden Fleece.

Aegeus: Aegeus was the king of Athens, and father of the great hero Theseus.

Aeneus: Aeneus was a Trojan prince and son-in-law of King Priam. He fought in the Trojan War, and when Troy fell, he escaped the burning city with his father. He founded a settlement in Italy, which eventually became the city of Rome. Aphrodite, goddess of love, was his mother.

Aeolus: Aeolus was the god of the winds.

Aeson: Aeson was the father of Jason and King of Iolcus until he was overthrown by his brother Pelias.

Agamemnon: Agamemnon was the king of Mycenae and high king of Greece. He lead the Greeks during the Trojan War. He is the brother of Menelaus.

Ajax: Ajax was a powerful warrior from Salamis, second only to Achilles. He was the tallest of the Greeks, standing a head and shoulders above his comrades. His skin was made impenetrable by being wrapped as an infant in the skin of the Nemean Lion.

Amazons: The Amazons were a race of female warriors, living mostly in Themiscyra, a region located in the north of Asia Minor on the coast of the Black Sea. It was said that they severed their left breasts so they wouldn't get in the way when firing a bow.

Andromeda: Andromeda was a princess in the far off city of Joppa, located in Syria. She was left as a sacrifice to a sea monster, but was rescued by Perseus, and returned with him to Greece as his wife.

Antigone: Antigone was the daughter of Oedipus and princess of Thebes. After her father was banished from the city she was put to death by for her defiance of the new king, Creon.

Antiope: Antiope was an Amazon queen who was abducted by Theseus, king of Athens, and became his wife.

Aphrodite: Aphrodite was the goddess of love and beauty. She was the wife of Hephestus and one of the Olympian gods.

Ares: Ares was the god of war and son of Zeus and Hera. He was one of the Olympian gods.

Argus: Argus was a creature possessing 100 eyes who Hera used as a watchdog.

Ariadne: Ariadne was the princess of Knossos and daughter of King Minos. She betrayed her father to help Theseus kill the Minotaur, and later became the wife of the god Dionysus.

Aristaeus: Aristaeus was a minor Thracian god of beekeeping. He was a satyr-like being who lived in the forest, and often had trouble controlling his amorous nature. He pursued Euridice, wife of Orpheus, causing her to step on a poisonous snake and receive a fatal bite.

Athena: Athena was the goddess of wisdom and strategy. She was the daughter of Zeus, and arose fully armored from his head. She always wore a helmet and carried a spear and shield, on which the head of Medusa was mounted. She was one of the Olympian gods.

Apollo: Apollo was the god of music, poetry, healing, and prophesy. He was the son of Zeus and the twin brother of Artemis. He founded the famous oracle of Delphi, and was one of the Olympian gods.

Artemis: Artemis was the goddess of the moon and of hunting and archery. She was the daughter of Zeus by the Titaness Leto, and the twin sister of Apollo. She was one of the Olympian gods.

Aesclepius: Aesclepius was the son of Apollo and the greatest healer of all time. He was an Argonaut, and was trained by the centaur Cheiron. His gift of healing was so great that eventually he could even revive the dead. Zeus could not allow this, so he killed the healer with a bolt of lightning. Later, however, Aesclepius was deified, and became the god of healing.

Atalanta: Atalanta was a virgin huntress, and the swiftest runner in all Greece.

Atlas: Atlas was a Titan who was punished by Zeus, and made to hold up the heavens for all eternity.

Bellerophon: Bellerophon was a brave warrior from Corinth. Banished from his homeland, he came to the region of Lycia where he captured and tamed the winged stallion Pegasus, then killed a monster known as the Chimera.

Calais: Calais was a son of Boreas, the north wind, and twin brother of Zetes. Both brothers had wings sprouting from their feet, allowing them to fly with unmatched speed. Calais and Zetes were both Argonauts.

Calchas: Calchas was a great prophet from Megara who advised the Greeks during the Trojan War.

Calypso: Calypso was an immortal nymph who lived on the remote island of Ogygia. She fell in love with Odysseus, and kept him captive on her island for many years.

Cassandra: Cassandra was a Trojan prophetess and daughter of King Priam. She was both blessed and cursed by the gods, for she could foretell the future without fail, but nobody would ever believe her prophecies.

Castor: Castor was the son of King Tyndareus of Sparta and the twin brother of Pollux. Both twins were Argonauts.

Cecrops: Cecrops was the earth-born founder of Athens. His lower body resembled that of a dragon.

Centaurs: The Centaurs were the offspring of Centarus, son of Ixion. They resembled horses but with the upper half of a man sprouting from the shoulders where the horse's neck and head would normally be. They were a barbaric race, driven mad by even the smell of wine. Many Centaurs lived in the vicinity of Mt. Pelion in Thessaly, and were ruled by Cheiron, who, unlike his Centaur brothers, was extremely wise.

Cerberus: Cerberus was a monstrous dog possessing three heads. He guarded the gates of the Underworld to ensure that no living being would enter, and that nobody, alive or dead, would leave.

Charon: Charon was the boatman who transported the dead across the river Styx into the Underworld.

Cheiron: Cheiron was a centaur who, unlike the others of his race, was extremely wise and learned. He was an expert healer, musician, and artist, and trained many heroes including Jason, and Achilles.

Chimera: The Chimera was a terrible monster who lived in Lycia. She resembled a lion with a long serpentine tail ending in a dragon's head, and the head of a goat sprouting from the middle of her back.

Circe: Circe was the daughter of Helios and the brother of Aeetes, king of Colchis. She was a sorceress who lived on the remote island of Aeaea, and delighted in transforming lost sailors into pigs.

Clytemnestra: Clytemnestra was the wife of Agamemnon and queen of Mycenae.

Creon: Creon was the brother of Jocasta and the uncle and brother-in-law of Oedipus, king of Thebes. After a civil war claimed both of Oedipus' sons, Creon became King.

Cretan Bull: The Cretan Bull, also known as the Marathon Bull, was given to King Minos of Knossos by the god Poseidon. He fathered the Minotaur by Minos' wife, was captured by Heracles, and later killed by Theseus in the vicinity of Athens.

Cronus: Cronus was a Titan, son of Gaea and Uranus. He was the father of the six original Olympian gods -- including Zeus -- by Rhea. He swallowed each of his children as they were born, but Rhea hid Zeus from him. Later, Zeus killed his father and became the ruler of the gods.

Cyclopes: The three original Cyclopes were sons of Uranus and Gaea. They sided with the gods in their battle with the Titans, and later became the assistants of Hephestus, and made Zeus' thunderbolts. Other Cyclopes lived on Sicily and nearby islands, but these were mostly shepherds -- violent and uncivilized.

Daedalus: Daedalus was a master craftsman, artist, and architect. He built the famous Labyrinth for King Minos of Knossos, and also built wings allowing him to fly.

Daphne: Daphne was a beautiful nymph -- a virgin huntress loved by the god Apollo. She fled from the god, but when she realized she could not escape, she transformed into a tree. Apollo made a crown from her leaves, which are now a symbol of victory in athletic events.

Deianara: Deianara was a huntress who married Heracles, and accidentally caused his death.

Demeter: Demeter was the goddess of agriculture and fertility. She was the sister of Zeus, the mother of Persephone, and one of the Olympian gods.

Deucalion: Deucalion was the son of Prometheus. He and his wife Pyrrha were the only human survivors of the great flood.

Dido: Dido was the queen and founder of the city of Carthage.

Diomedes: Diomedes was one of the strongest of the Greek warriors to fight in the Trojan War.

Dionysus: Dionysus was the god of joy and revelry and the inventor of wine. He was the son of Zeus, and was raised and tutored by Silenus,the wise satyr. Dionysus' most faithful followers were the satyrs and the Maenads, wild women subject to bouts of frenzied passion. Dionysus was called "twice born" because he was attacked and torn limb from limb by cruel giants -- Zeus killed the giants and ate the fallen god's remains, and later fathered Dionysus a second time.

Dragons: Dragons were giant snakelike monsters. Many dragons appear in Greek Mythology -- among them, Ladon, who guarded the golden apples; Python, a monster slain by Apollo; and other nameless dragons slain by Cadmus and Jason.

Eris: Eris was the goddess of discord and strife. It was she who left the golden apple marked "for the fairest" among the guests at the wedding of Thetis and Peleus. Athena, Aphrodite, and Hera all claimed the prize. Paris was asked to judge the goddesses, and he chose Aphrodite. As a reward she promised Paris the most beautiful woman in the world. These events eventually lead to the abduction of Helen and the Trojan War.

Eros: Eros was the god of love and desire, emotions which he could impose on any being, mortal or immortal, with his bow and arrows. Eros appeared as a beautiful youth with wings sprouting from his back.

Eurystheus: Eurystheus was a king of Mycenae who sent Heracles on his famous 12 labors.

Eurydice: Eurydice was a lovely nymph from Thrace and the wife of Orpheus. When she died of a fatal snake bite, Orpheus attempted to bring her back from the Underworld, but failed.

Fire-Breathing Bull: There were two of these monstrous bulls, both with feet of bronze and breath of fire. They were owned by Aeetes, king of Colchis, who forced Jason to yoke them and plow a field with dragon's teeth.

Furies: The Furies were three goddesses, born from the blood of Uranus, whose job it was to avenge blood crimes, especially the murder of one's father or mother. They pursued Orestes for killing his mother Clytemnestra, and tormented him to the brink of insanity. Another duty of the Furies was to punish those condemned by Zeus to Tartarus, a region of the Underworld.

Gaea: Gaea was the first being to emerge from Chaos. She was the goddess of the earth, and mother of the Titans, the giants, the Cyclopes and many others.

Geryon: Geryon was a giant with three heads and torsos, and was the king of the far-off land of Erytheia.

Giants: The Giants were a race of gigantic men with legs that ended in serpent-like tails. They were sons of Gaea, and attempted to overthrow Zeus and the Olympian gods.

Gorgons: The gorgons were three sisters with snakes for hair, claws of bronze, and wings of gold. They had huge tongues which hung out between their tusks, and their faces were so horrible that anyone who looked upon them would be turned to stone. The three gorgons were Stheno, Euryale, and Medusa. Unlike her sisters, Medusa was mortal, and was killed by Perseus.

Graiai: The Graiai were three sisters, wise old crones -- grey-haired from birth. They had only one eye and one tooth to share between them.

Hades: Hades was the brother of Zeus and the son of Cronus. He was the god of the Underworld and the dead. His wife was Persephone, daughter of Demeter. His watchdog was the three-headed Cerberus.

Harpies: The Harpies were monsters that resembled filthy birds with human female heads. In addition to their random snatching away of innocents and befouling of food, they also acted as the "hounds of Zeus" and were sent by him at times to torment transgressors.

Hecatoncheires: The Hecatoncheires were 100-armed giants, sons of Gaea and Uranus, who guarded the gates of Tartarus in the Underworld.

Hector: Hector was the son of King Priam, and the strongest warrior on the side of Troy during the Trojan War. He was killed by Achilles who dragged his body around the walls of Troy, but later surrendered it to Priam.

Helen: Helen was the daughter of Zeus by Leda, queen of Sparta, and was thought to be the most beautiful woman in the world. She was married to Meneleus, but was later abducted by Paris, prince of Troy, which is what started the Trojan War.

Helios: Helios was one of the Titans and the god of the sun. He drove his sun chariot across the sky every day.

Hephestus: Hephestus was the god of blacksmiths and is the greatest craftsman among the gods. He has made many fantastic objects and built glorious structures, including the homes of the gods on Mt. Olympus. He was the son of Hera, who cast him out of Olympus because of his deformity, but was later allowed to return. He was the husband of Aphrodite and one of the Olympian gods.

Hera: Hera was the queen of the gods and the goddess of marriage and the protector of women. She was the wife of Zeus and was extremely jealous of his many affairs, sometimes persecuting his children throughout their entire lives.

Heracles: Heracles was the son of Zeus and the greatest hero of all time. So great was he that upon his death he was made an immortal god. He wasn't perfect, however -- he was subject to fits of insanity and rage, and in one such instance he killed his own wife. Heracles was most famous for performing his twelve labors. On these labors he collected two powerful weapons: the impenetrable skin of the Nemean Lion, and the venom of the Hydra in which he dipped his deadly arrows.

Hermes: Hermes was the god of messengers, travelers, and merchants. He was the son of Zeus and one of the cleverest tricksters of all time. He acted as a messenger to Zeus and also shepherded the spirits of the dead into the Underworld. Hermes was the most recognizable of the gods with his winged sandals and helmet, and his Caduceus, a wand intertwined with snakes. Hermes is one of the Olympian gods.

Hestia: Hestia was the goddess of the hearth and the protector of homes and cities. She was the sister of Zeus and one of the Olympian gods.

Hippolyte: Hippolyte was an Amazon queen. She wore a magnificent belt, a treasure prized by many -- The theft of this object was one of Heracles' twelve labors.

Hydra: The Hydra was a horrible nine-headed monster who lived in a marsh near Lerna. Whenever one of its heads was cut off, two would grow in its place unless the wound was immediately cauterized. The Hydra's venom was one of the most deadly poisons known to man. One of Heracles' tasks was to kill this creature.

Hylus: Hylus was a beautiful youth who accompanied Heracles on the Argo during Jason's quest for the Golden Fleece. Once when the Argonauts stopped to gather supplies, Hylus was carried off by a sea nymph, and Heracles stayed behind to search for him.

Icarus: Icarus was the son of Daedalus, the great inventor. When Daedalus built wings in order to escape the island of Crete, Icarus ignored his father's warning and flew too close to the sun. The sun's heat melted the wax which held the wings together, and Icarus plunged into the sea.

Iphigeneia: Iphigeneia was the oldest daughter of King Agamemnon. When Agamemnon's fleet was stranded at Aulis without favorable winds, Artemis demanded the sacrifice of Iphigeneia before she would allow the Greeks to sail on to Troy. Artemis saved Iphigeneia at the last minute, and made her a priestess at her temple in Tauria.

Jason: Jason was the son of Aeson, king of Iolcus. When Pelias seized the throne, Jason was brought to Cheiron, the wise centaur, who raised him to manhood. Jason returned, but was sent by Pelias on the famous quest for the Golden Fleece. Many of Greece's greatest heroes joined Jason on his quest, even the great Heracles.

Jocasta: Jocasta was the wife of King Laius of Thebes and the mother, and later the wife, of Oedipus. When she discovered that she had married her own son, she killed herself, and Oedipus put out his own eyes, and was banished from Thebes.

Ladon: Ladon was a gigantic dragon who guarded the Golden Apples of the Hesperides, and was killed by Heracles.

Laestygonians: The Laestygonians were a race of cannibalistic giants encountered by Odysseus on his travels.

Laius: Laius was the father of Oedipus and king of Thebes.

Leto: Leto was a titaness and the mother of Apollo and Artemis by Zeus.

Maenads: The Maenads were female followers of Dionysus who were subject to fits of frenzied rage, and would tear any creature they encountered to shreds.

Marsyas: Marsyas was a satyr and a brilliant musician. He claimed to be a greater musician than Apollo himself. For this crime of hubris, Marsyas was skinned alive.

Medea: Medea was a sorceress and daughter of King Aeetes of Colchis. She betrayed her father and helped Jason steal the Golden Fleece. She returned with Jason to Greece, but Jason soon left her for another woman. Medea killed her two children by Jason, and escaped to Athens. In Athens she tried to kill Theseus, and was banished. She eventually returned home and helped her father regain his throne.

Medusa: Medusa was one of the three Gorgons, hideous monsters who could turn men to stone with a single glance. She was the only Gorgon of the three who was mortal. Perseus killed Medusa, and gave her head to Athena, who placed it on her shield. When Medusa was killed, the winged stallion, Pegasus was born from her blood.

Meleager. Meleager was an Argonaut and killed the monstrous Calydonian Boar. He was destined to die when a certain piece of wood that was on the pyre at his birth was completely burned away. His mother took the timber off the fire and hid it away, but later burned it in retribution for the death of her brothers.

Meneleus: Meneleus was the brother of Agamemnon and the king of Sparta. His wife was Helen, who ran away with Paris to Troy, causing the Trojan War.

Midas: Midas was a Phrygian king and the richest man in the world. He once kidnapped Silenus, then restored him to Dionysus. His reward for this was the golden touch. Whatever Midas touched would turn into solid gold. He was overjoyed at first, but soon learned he couldn't eat or drink, for as soon as the food touched his lips it would transform into gold. Dionysus took back the gift, and Midas renounced his wealth.

Minos: Minos was the most powerful king of Knossos. He once ruled the entire Aegean with his powerful navy, and even demanded an annual tribute of seven youths and seven maidens from Athens to feed the Minotaur, a bull-headed monster who he kept imprisoned in an intricate Labyrinth.

Minotaur: The Minotaur was a monster who resembles a man with the head of a bull. He was imprisoned by King Minos in a Labyrinth designed by Daedalus. Once a year, Athens sent a tribute of seven youths and seven maidens to feed the foul beast -- until Theseus finally killed it.

Nemean lion: The Nemean Lion was a monstrous lion whose skin was immune to all weapons. Heracles killed the monster by strangling it, then removed its skin using the beast's own claws, and wore it as an impenetrable cloak.

Neoptolomus: Neoptolomus was the son of Achilles. He joined the Trojan War in its final year, and killed King Priam during the sack of Troy.

Nessus: Nessus was a centaur who worked as a ferryman by a river near Aetolia. He tried to ravish Heracles' wife, Deianara, but Heracles shot him with arrows poisoned with the Hydra's venom. Nessus gave Deianara some of his blood, telling her to use it as a love potion should Heracles' affections ever turn elsewhere. But Nessus tricked her. When she finally did use the love potion, The Hydra's venom caused Heracles to die a painful death.

Nestor: Nestor was the king of Pylos, and the oldest man to fight in the Trojan War. His prudent advice often influenced King Agamemnon, leader of the expedition.

Nymphs: Nymphs were beautiful female spirits who lived in forests, bodies of water, and other natural settings.

Ocean: Ocean was a titan and the god of the ocean.

Odysseus: Odysseus was the king of Ithaca, and was well known for his cunning and eloquence. He fought in the Trojan War, and invented the idea of the Trojan Horse, which won the war for the Greeks. On his way home he was lost at sea for ten years, and encountered many strange and terrible creatures such as Polyphemus, Circe, and Scylla and Charybdis.

Oedipus: Oedipus was a king of Thebes who unwittingly killed his own father and married his mother. When he discovered what he had done, he blinded himself, and was banished from

Thebes. Oedipus was also known for solving the riddle of the Sphinx, a victory which won him the throne of Thebes.

Oracle of Delphi: The Oracle was a priestess of Apollo at his temple in Delphi. Her gift of prophesy was sought far and wide.

Orestes: Orestes was the son of Agamemnon. In revenge for his father's murder, he killed his mother, Clytemnestra, and was pursued by the Furies for his crime.

Orion: Orion was the greatest hunter of all time. So great, in fact, that he attracted the affections of Artemis, goddess of the hunt. When Orion bragged that he was going to hunt down every animal on the face of the earth, Gaea sent a scorpion to deliver a deadly sting, and Orion met his fate.

Orpheus: Orpheus was the son of one of the Muses, goddesses of the arts, and was the greatest musician of all time. His wife was a nymph named Euridice. When she died of a fatal snake bite, Orpheus went to the underworld to bring her back. Charmed by his music, Hades agreed on the condition that, on his way back to the surface, he never look back to see if she was truly following him. Orpheus couldn't resist looking back and Euridice was pulled back into Hades' realm forever.

Orthrus: Orthrus was a two-headed dog who guarded the cattle of Geryon.

Pan: Pan was the god of nature and shepherds. He resembled a satyr, with his horns and goat-like hooves. He was the son of Hermes, and invented the Syrinx, or panpipes.

Pandora: Pandora was the first woman, and was made by Hephestus as a mate for Prometheus' creation, the first man. Pandora opened a box which contained all manner of plagues and curses, and in so doing doomed mankind to endless suffering.

Paris: Paris was a prince of Troy, and the brother of Hector. He awarded a golden apple to Aphrodite, and in return, he was promised the most beautiful woman in the world. This woman was Helen, wife of Meneleus, king of Sparta. Paris took her back to Troy, thus starting a turn of events that would lead to the famous Trojan War.

Patroclus: Patroclus was the dearest friend of Achilles, and was killed by Hector during the Trojan War.

Pegasus: Pegasus was a fabulous winged stallion, born from the blood of Medusa when she was beheaded by Perseus. Bellerophon managed to capture Pegasus, and rode him into battle against a monster called the Chimera.

Peleus: Peleus was one of the Argonauts, and later became the father of Achilles by the goddess Thetis.

Pelias: Pelias killed Jason's father, Aeson, and became king of Iolcus. He sent Jason on his famous quest for the Golden Fleece.

Penthesileia: Penthesileia was an Amazon queen who fought on the side of the Trojans during the Trojan War. She was killed by Achilles.

Persephone: Persephone was the daughter of Demeter, and was abducted by Hades, who made her his queen. She spent part of the year with her mother on Mt. Olympus, and part of the year with Hades in the Underworld. Demeter's sorrow at her daughter's absence caused winter to come every year.

Perseus: Perseus was the son of Zeus, and a great hero who killed Medusa the Gorgon. When an infant, he was thrown into the sea with his mother by his grandfather who feared a prophesy that his grandson would one day kill him. Perseus also founded the city of Mycenae.

Phineus: Phineus was a blind seer who was tormented by harpies. Jason and the Argonauts chased the harpies away, freeing Phineus from his curse.

Pholus: Pholus, like Cheiron, was a wise centaur. He was the son of Silenus, and was accidentally killed by Heracles.

Pollux: Pollux was the son of Zeus and the twin brother of Castor. Unlike his brother, he was immortal.

Poseidon: Poseidon was the god of the sea and earthquakes. He always carried a trident, or three-pronged spear and was the brother of Zeus and Hades, the creator of horses, and one of the Olympian gods.

Polyphemus: Polyphemus was a cruel and barbaric Cyclops, and was the son of Poseidon. He captured Odysseus and his men on their way home from Troy, and would have eaten them all one by one, but Odysseus made him drunk on wine and blinded him.

Priam: Priam was the king of Troy during the Trojan War. He was the father of Hector, Paris, Cassandra, and many others.

Prometheus: Prometheus, a titan, was assigned the task of creating all living things. His favorite creation, however was mankind. He loved them so much that he stole the gift of fire from the gods and gave it to his creations. For this, Zeus punished him by having him chained to a mountain and eternally tormented by an eagle. He was later released by Heracles.

Proteus: Proteus was a shape-changing sea god who lived in Egypt and tended Poseidon's herd of seals. He was very wise, but would only impart his wisdom to those who could capture him, and keep hold despite his many transformations.

Psyche: Psyche was a very beautiful woman who became the wife of Eros, god of love.

Pygmalion: A king of Cyprus, and a great artist. He constructed a statue of Aphrodite that was so realistic that he fell in love with it. In answer to his prayers, Aphrodite brought the statue to life.

Pyrrha: Pyrrha was the wife of Deucalion, and one of the only two survivors of the great flood.

Python: Python was a dragon killed by Apollo. It was at the site of this battle that Apollo established the city of Delphi and his famous oracle.

Rhea: Rhea was a titaness, the wife of Cronus, and the mother of the Olympian gods.

Sarpedon: Sarpedon was a son of Zeus by Europa who lived in Lycia and fought with the Trojans during the Trojan War.

Satyrs: Satyrs were male woodland creatures resembling snub-nosed men with horns and horse-like tails. They were followers of Dionysus and were fond of wine, music, dancing, and the company of nymphs.

Scylla: Scylla was a 6-headed sea monster who devoured sailors. She lived in a cave in the Strait of Messina, between Sicily and Italy, who devoured sailors. On the other side of the strait was Charybdis, a great whirlpool.

Silenus: Silenus was a wise old satyr who was the dearest friend and tutor of Dionysus. He was fat , bald, and often drunk, but he had great powers of prophesy.

Sirens: The Sirens were monsters who lured ships to their doom with their enchanting songs. They resembled birds with the heads of beautiful women.

Sphinx: The Sphinx was a monster who resembled a winged lion with the head of a woman. She would ask a riddle of her intended victims, and kill those who failed to answer it.

Stymphalian Birds: The Stymphalian Birds were monster birds who could throw arrow-like feathers. They lived in the Stymphalian marsh in Arcadia.

Syrinx: Syrinx was a beautiful nymph and huntress who became the unwilling object of Pan's affection. She transformed into a clump of reeds in order to escape him. From the reeds, Pan made his famous panpipes.

Talos: Talos was a giant of solid bronze made by Hephestus and given to King Minos of Crete. Talos guarded the shores of Crete, throwing stones at any ship that came too close. He had one weak spot on his ankle which, if pierced,would cause a special fluid to run out, rendering him immobile.

Teiresias: Teiresias was a blind prophet, considered the greatest seer of all time.

Thetis: Thetis was a minor sea goddess. She was married to the former Argonaut, Peleus, and was the mother of Achilles, the greatest of the Greek heroes to take part in the Trojan War.

Titans: The Titans were a race of giants, the offspring of Gaea and Uranus. They once ruled the heavens under Cronus, but Zeus defeated them and became the new ruler of the gods. A few titans sided with Zeus, and still maintain important positions. Among them are Helios, Ocean, and Prometheus.

Typhon: Typhon was a powerful dragon-like monster, the son of Gaea. He attacked the gods, driving them into hiding, but Zeus eventually defeated him and imprisoned him in Tartarus.

Telemachus: Telemachus was the son of Odysseus by Penelope.

Theseus: Theseus was a great hero and the son of Aegeus of Athens. He was best known for killing the bull-headed Minotaur of Knossos. After his father's death, he became ruler of Athens and ruled wisely for many years.

Uranus: Uranus was the god of the heavens, the offspring and husband of Gaea. With her, he fathered many children such as the Titans and the Cyclopes. He was defeated and overthrown by his son Cronus.

Zetes: Zetes was a son of Boreas, the north wind, and twin brother of Calais. Both brothers had wings sprouting from their feet, allowing them to fly with unmatched speed. Calais and Zetes were both Argonauts.

Zeus: Zeus was the god of the sky and thunder and the all-powerful king of the gods on Mt. Olympus. He was married to his sister, Hera, who was jealous of his many affairs with other goddesses and mortal women. He fathered many of the Olympian gods as well as a few mortal heroes such as Perseus and Horacles. Zeus was the son of the titan, Cronus, who had swallowed all of his older brothers and sisters. Zeus defeated Cronus, freed his siblings, and became the ruler of the gods. His greatest weapons were his thunderbolts which were forged by Hephestus.

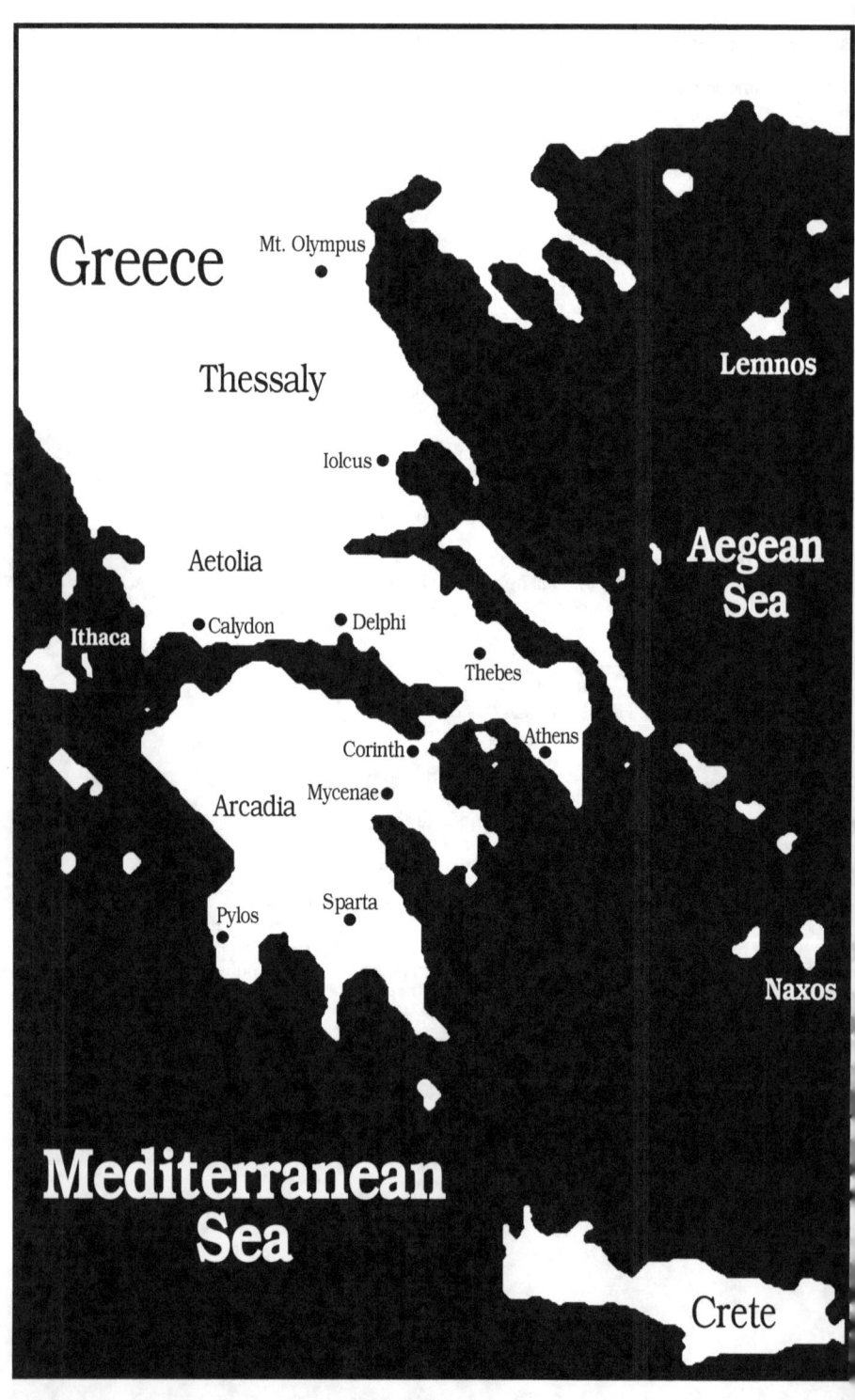

Greece

Mt. Olympus

Thessaly

Iolcus

Aetolia

Ithaca

Calydon

Delphi

Thebes

Aegean
Sea

Lemnos

Corinth

Athens

Arcadia

Mycenae

Pylos

Sparta

Naxos

Mediterranean
Sea

Crete

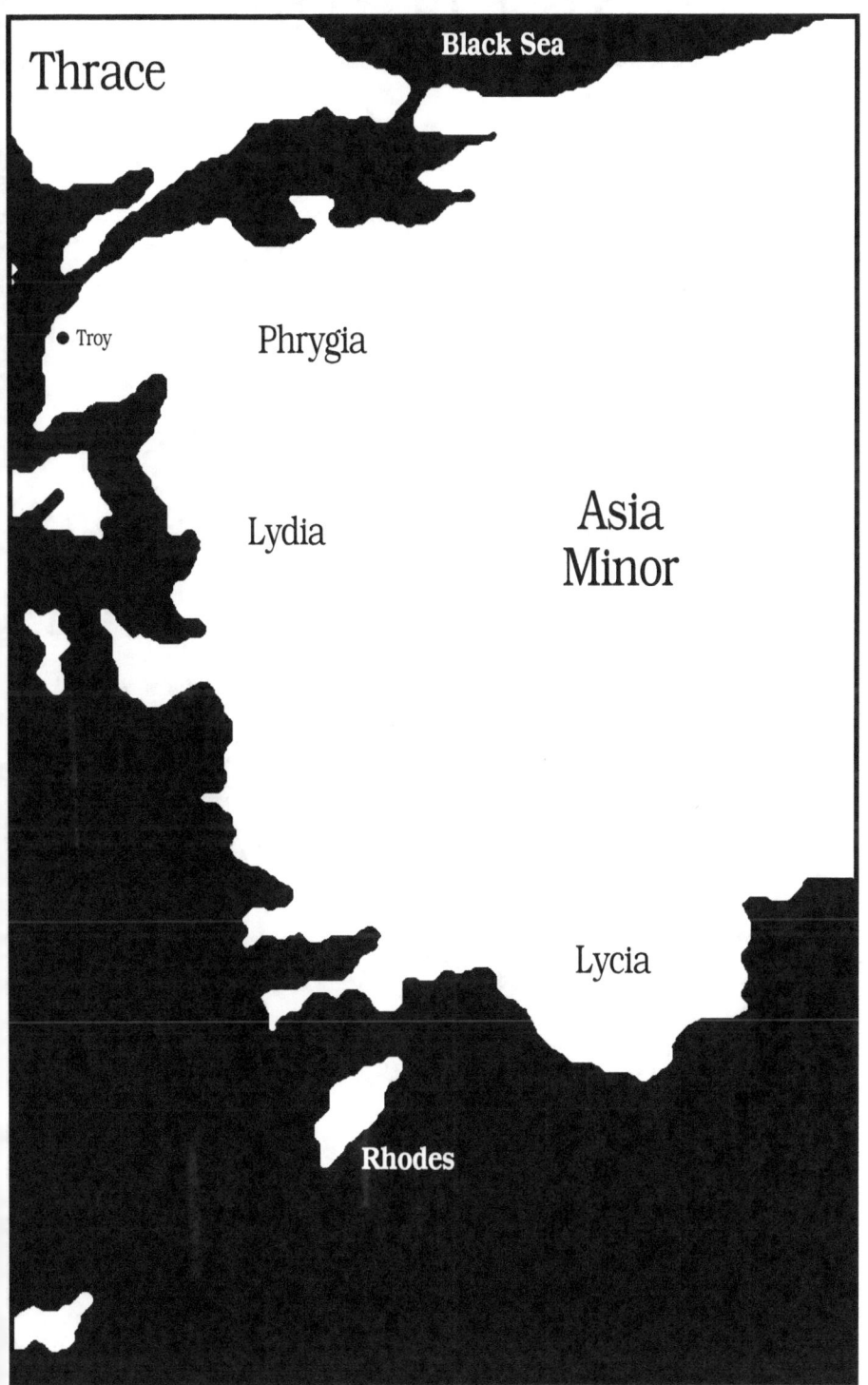

SKETCHES

One of my first drawings of Silenus

HEY GOOD LOOKIN'

The Chimera

ACHILLES

Various Monsters

An Amazon

Concepts for Heracles

Some idea sketches
of Polyphemus

Cheiron the Centaur

Concepts
for Zeus

Ideas for Medusa

Ideas for
The Minotaur

Various heroes

Satyr
Drawings

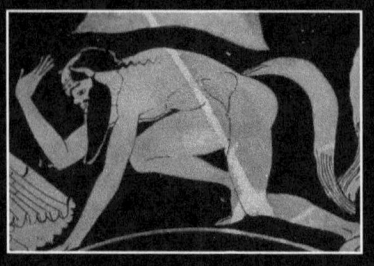

I hope you enjoyed *The Grand Tour of Greek Mythology*. If so, please check out my *Satyr* comic books which can be ordered at the address below.

Satyr follows the adventures of Silenus, the wisest of the satyrs, and his band of fun-loving creatures who live on the remote island of Nysa. Silenus and the satyrs often show off their en-cyclop-edic knowledge of Greek myths by recounting the famous tales -- but with a twist. In their versions, the satyrs get involved -- helping heroes and gods alike to achieve their mythic tasks.

Don't miss these pun-packed, satyr-ized adventures! Order *Satyr* today! Also check out the cool Satyr T-shirt. Quantities are limited, so don't wait!

Join the SATYR'S FACTION! Just send your name, address, and e-mail and receive periodic *Satyr* updates via e-mail!

satyrsfaction@aol.com

www.satyrplayproductions.com

More Fine Products Are Available From Satyr Play!

Check out the Our Website:
www.satyrplayproductions.com
Satyrsfaction@aol.com